DATE DUE

GAYLORD

PRINTED IN U.S.A.

DES PLAINES, ILLINOIS 60016

D1528723

Jewish Holidays

BY
Mary Turck

CRESTWOOD HOUSE
New York

Library of Congress Cataloging-in-Publication Data

Turck, Mary.
  Jewish holidays

  p. cm. — (Holidays)
  Includes bibliographical references.
  Summary: Discusses the origins of traditions surrounding the Jewish holidays.
  ISBN 0-89686-502-9
  1. Fasts and feasts—Judaism—Juvenile literature. [1. Fasts and feasts—Judaism.] I. Title. II. Series:
Holidays
BM690.T86   1990   89-25398
296.4'3—dc20   CIP
                                                                                 AC

Photo Credits
Cover: Journalism Services: Chris Marona
Peter Arnold, Inc.: (Tompix) 4; (Yoram Lehmann) 24, 32, 35, 42; (Erika Stone) 7; (Dan Porges) 8, 11, 25,
    27, 28; (Cecile Brunswick) 15, 36; (Barbara Pfeffer) 33, 39; (Martha Cooper) 44
Journalism Services: (Richard Derk) 16; (Chris Marona) 41
DRK Photo: (Don & Pat Valenti) 18
Devaney Stock Photos: 21, 40
Berg & Associates: (Arnold J. Kaplan) 38

CRESTWOOD HOUSE

Macmillan Publishing Company
866 Third Avenue
New York, NY 10022
Collier Macmillan Canada, Inc.

Printed in the United States

First Edition

10 9 8 7 6 5 4 3 2 1

Contents

To Be Jewish Is to Celebrate
  Different Ways to Be Jewish 5
  Queen of the Week—The Sabbath 8
Seasons of Celebration
  Rosh Hashanah—The New Year 10
  Yom Kippur—The Day of Atonement 12
  Sukkot—The Harvest Festival 14
  Hanukkah—Feast of Lights 16
  Purim—Costumes and Stories. 19
  Pesach—Passover 22
  The Seder—Special Meal and Story 24
  Shavuot—The Feast of Weeks 29
  Days of Mourning 30
Life Cycle Celebrations
  Naming the Baby 31
  Bar Mitzvah, Bat Mitzvah. 33
  Weddings 34
  When Someone Dies—Sitting Shiva 37
Blessings Old and New. 39
For Further Reading 46
Index 47

The Passover seder is an important Jewish celebration that remembers the end of slavery for biblical Jews in Egypt.

To Be Jewish Is to Celebrate

Different Ways To Be Jewish

Sarah's family celebrates the Sabbath every week. They go to synagogue on Saturday mornings and say prayers in Hebrew. Sarah started going to Hebrew school in third grade. She goes three afternoons every week, after her regular school.

Nathan goes to Hebrew school, too. Nathan's family doesn't celebrate the Sabbath. They go to temple only once or twice during the year for the High Holy Days. Most of the prayers at their temple are said in English. Nathan looks forward to being thirteen and having his bar mitzvah. This special ceremony for Jewish boys welcomes them to adulthood.

Paula's grandmother tells Paula stories about escaping from Germany. Most of her grandmother's family was killed during the Holocaust because they were Jewish. Paula doesn't go to temple. Her family doesn't celebrate any Jewish holidays.

Sarah, Nathan, and Paula are all proud to be Jews. But each is Jewish in a different way. What does it mean to be Jewish? Does it have to do with religion, nationality, race, or language?

More than 3,000 years ago, tribes of people living in the Near East joined together as a nation. They were related to one another. They shared the same religion. They lived in the same small country. They celebrated the same holy days. They ate the same foods and lived by the same rules.

Now the descendants of those people are scattered around the world. Many live in Israel. But just as many live in the United States. Others live in Honduras, Ethiopia, the Soviet Union, France—in nearly every country of the world.

Some Jews are white and some are black, such as the Falasha from Ethiopia. Many Jews learn Hebrew, but many more do not understand it. Jews from Germany and some parts of eastern Europe speak Yiddish. Yiddish is a mixture of German and Hebrew. Jews from eastern Europe are called Ashkenazic Jews. Jews from Spain and Portugal speak Ladino, a mixture of Spanish and Hebrew. They are called Sephardic Jews.

To make matters even more complicated, some people become Jewish. They believe in and study the Jewish religion. Then they go through a special procedure called conversion. But conversion is relatively uncommon in Judaism. Jews do not look for converts. Most people who convert to Judaism do so because they marry Jews.

On the other hand, some people who are Jewish don't believe in the religious aspect of Judaism at all. They consider themselves cultural or secular Jews.

Holidays and traditions are an important part of culture. Jewish holidays all began as holy days. Today, some parts of holiday celebrations are still religious. Other parts have to do with honoring moments in Jewish history or celebrating freedom and courage. And still other parts have to do with good food and fun. Many non-religious or non-observant Jews celebrate the holidays, too. Because Hebrew is the official religious language of the Jews, Jewish holidays have Hebrew names.

Jews in all parts of the world celebrate the same holidays—but they celebrate in different ways. In this book, we will look at candles, bread, wine, Hanukkah gelt, eating outdoors, wearing costumes, and at lots of other important parts of Jewish culture and tradition.

An Orthodox Jew in Israel reads the notices displayed for his community.

Queen of the Week— The Sabbath

On Friday afternoons, Sarah hurries home from school. She loves to help her mother make challah. Actually, her mother made the bread dough for the challah early in the day, before she cleaned house. Now the bread dough is ready to be braided. Sarah helps to braid it. Then she brushes it with egg white and sprinkles it with poppy seeds. Finally the challah bakes in the oven. Sarah and her family enjoy challah every Friday night as they celebrate Shabbat.

Challah is the traditional bread prepared and braided for each sabbath celebration.

Shabbat or *Shabbos* is the Hebrew word for Sabbath, or holy day. The Sabbath begins as the sun sets on Friday evening. It lasts until sunset on Saturday. Religious Jews, like Sarah's family, celebrate it every week. "Keep holy the Lord's Day" is one of the commandments God gave to Moses. The Lord's Day is the last day of the week. God rested then, the Bible says, after making the world.

Just before sundown, Sarah's family gathers around the dinner table. Set with sparkling glasses and snowy napkins, the table is beautiful. Sarah's mother says a prayer of blessing and thanks as she lights the candles. Then Sarah's father says a prayer over the wine. This prayer over the wine is called the kiddush. Sarah's mother says another prayer as they share the challah.

The Sabbath is called the "queen of the week" because it makes every week special. The heart of Jewish tradition is in the home and that is where the Sabbath is celebrated. Sarah's family also goes to synagogue to pray on Saturday morning. But the most important part of the Sabbath is the family celebration.

On Saturday, the members of Sarah's family don't do any work. Instead they attend Sabbath services, study holy books, or visit family. That is their way of keeping the Lord's Day holy. Sarah's family belongs to an Orthodox synagogue. They are quite observant —that is, they follow the religious laws and traditions closely.

The laws about keeping the Sabbath can be very strict. Some Orthodox Jews follow laws that say they may not cook, drive a car, handle money, or even turn on lights on the Sabbath. Hasidic Jews are also strict about their practices. They try to dress and live much as their founders in Poland did three centuries ago. Other groups are not quite as strict, though.

Jesse's family belongs to a Reform temple. This is another branch of Judaism in the United States. While Orthodox Judaism uses only

Hebrew prayers, Reform Judaism uses a lot of English prayers. Other branches of Judaism in the United States are called Conservative and Reconstructionist. Some Jews call their place of worship a temple. Others call it a synagogue or a shul.

Seasons of Celebration

Rosh Hashanah— The New Year

"Happy New Year! It's the first day of the month of Tishri in the year 5570!"

In the Jewish calendar, months and years are calculated differently than in the familiar Roman calendar, which we use most of the time. The first day of the month of Tishri in 5570 in the Jewish calendar is September 30, 1989 in the Roman calendar! The Jewish calendar is based on the cycles of the moon. This means Jewish holidays fall on different days in the Roman calendar every year.

Rosh Hashanah is the beginning of the new year. It is celebrated for two days at the beginning of the High Holy Days. The ten days known as the High Holy Days are also called the Days of Awe. The most important celebrations take place in synagogue or temple. The shofar, or ram's horn, is a special part of Rosh Hashanah. It is sounded several times during Rosh Hashanah and the Days of Awe.

Sarah finds the synagogue service very long. She prefers the festive family meal. Her favorite part is dipping apples in honey. Eating

The shofar, or ram's horn, is sounded several times during Rosh
Hashanah.

honey is a way of hoping for a new year that is good and sweet. Sometimes the challah is made in a round shape for Rosh Hashanah. Then it looks like a crown for God. On the second night of Rosh Hashanah, Sarah's family eats a "new" fruit. This year Sarah picked kiwi as the funny fruit; last year she chose a mango.

Another New Year's custom Sarah likes is called tashlikh. This means "throwing your sins away." Sarah and her family observe tashlikh by going to a river or lake and turning their pockets inside out. Then they throw bread crumbs in the water to symbolize the discarding of their sins. This is a way of making a new start in a new year. Happy New Year wishes are only one part of the Days of Awe. Planning to live a better life is an even more important part.

Yom Kippur— The Day of Atonement

A legend says that God hears the shofar on Rosh Hashanah. When it sounds, the Book of Life is opened. Every person's name is written in this book. God has listed all the good and bad things that each one has done in the past year next to his or her name. The Book of Life stays open during the Days of Awe. This gives people a chance for a new start. They can be sorry for bad things they have done and try to make amends. Then God will put a "good signature" next to their name. That means a clean start for the new year ahead. The Book of Life is closed again when the shofar sounds at the end of Yom Kippur.

As Rosh Hashanah begins the Days of Awe, Yom Kippur ends them. Yom Kippur is the most solemn day in the year. It begins with

Kol Nidre, an evening prayer service, and ends the next evening with another prayer service. For the very observant, there are three other prayer services in between.

Yom Kippur is also a day of fasting. A good meal is eaten before sundown on the evening when Yom Kippur begins. Then there is no eating or drinking until the next night. After the next day's ending prayers and after sundown, a light meal finishes the day. Another Yom Kippur custom is a special candle. If a close relative has died, the family lights a candle in memory of the relative. The memorial candle burns all through the day.

No leather shoes should be worn on Yom Kippur. Nor should there be any eating, drinking, nor any kind of love-making. These rules remind people that Yom Kippur is not a day for comfort or pleasure. Like the Sabbath, Yom Kippur is a day when no work should be done. Unlike the Sabbath, it is not a day for enjoyment.

The Days of Awe and Yom Kippur are special times for pledging money to help the poor. Tzedekah—charity—is an important part of Jewish practice all year long. Some Jewish families keep a little box called a pischke in the kitchen. When something good happens—like a baby being born—they put in some coins. When there is enough money in the pischke, it is given to help the poor.

On Yom Kippur, people reflect on their sins and failings. On this day, God gives them a chance for a new beginning. The past can be forgiven and forgotten. As the day ends, the shofar sounds for the last time.

Sukkot—
The Harvest Festival

Almost as soon as Yom Kippur ends, the next holiday begins. Sukkot is a festival celebrating the harvest. It begins on Tishri 15 and lasts for a week in late September or October each year. *Sukkah* is a Hebrew word that means hut. (*Sukkot* is the plural form—*huts.*) Also called the Festival of Booths, it is celebrated by building a small hut or booth (the sukkah) in the backyard.

One story says that these huts are like the tents in the desert that the Jewish people lived in thousands of years ago. Thus, Sukkot is a celebration of the Lord's care for the people in the desert. Another story says they are like the huts that workers built in the fields to live in during harvest time. Thus, Sukkot is a celebration of the harvest.

Each hut has four walls and a roof of branches. The roof must be solid enough to give shade from the sun. It must also be open enough to see the stars through it at night. Branches from four kinds of trees—citron, palm, myrtle, and willow—are also needed. These branches are held and shaken during the blessing prayers.

On the first night, the whole family eats dinner in the sukkah. Depending on the weather, people sometimes study, sleep, or talk and visit in it. Sometimes special chairs are set for "honored guests"— people from the Torah like Abraham, Moses, and Isaac. While there are prayers at the synagogue or temple for Sukkot, most of the celebration and prayer takes place at home. During the seven days of Sukkot, people visit one another's huts and eat cake and drink wine together.

In preparation for the Festival of Booths, a man builds a hut, known as a sukkah. During the holiday, family members will eat, visit, and even sleep in the sukkah.

A young boy lights a menorah, a nine-branched candle holder, used in the celebration of Hanukkah.

Hanukkah— Feast of Lights

Hanukkah is celebrated every year in December. It celebrates a miracle that happened more than 2,000 years ago. At that time, the most important religious place for Jews was the great temple in Jerusalem. But Jews in Israel were living under Syrian-Greek rule.

16

A new king, Antiochus Epiphanes, ordered that Jews stop practicing their own religion. This king stole many beautiful things from the Jerusalem Temple. Then he put up a statue of a Greek god in the most holy place.

The Maccabee family led the Jewish people in a rebellion. They fought against the Greek army and won. Then they cleansed and rededicated the Temple and relit the special Temple lamp. This lamp was kept burning day and night. But at the time of the rededication, there was only enough oil to last one day. By a miracle, the oil kept the lamp burning for eight days and nights until more oil could be prepared!

The Feast of Lights — Hanukkah — celebrates this miracle. Hanukkah is a feast celebrating freedom, especially the freedom to believe and practice one's own religion. On Hanukkah, Jews light a menorah. The Hanukkah menorah is a special nine-branched candle holder. On the first night, one candle is lit; on the second night, two candles; and so on until all eight candles are lit. The ninth candle is the one used to light the others. It is called the *shamas*, or helper.

Hanukkah is not as important a holiday as the Days of Awe or Passover, but it is great fun. Every night as the candles are burning, the family gathers for songs and prayers. Family and friends often give Hanukkah gifts to each other. Hanukkah gelt, which means Hanukkah money, can be a coin or chocolate candy wrapped in gold-colored foil.

Children love to play games with the dreidl. A dreidl is a four-sided top with Hebrew letters on each side. Players win or lose depending on which letter is up when the top stops. Dreidl games are usually played with candy, nuts, or raisins. Some families have board games to play with the dreidl.

Latkes—potato pancakes—are a special treat on Hanukkah. They are fried in oil and remind people of the oil that burned in the Jerusalem Temple lamp for eight days. In Israel, and among the Sephardic Jews, people eat fried doughnuts—sufganiyot—for the same reason.

Part of Hanukkah is giving and receiving gifts.

Some non-Jewish people call Hanukkah "the Jewish Christmas." That is not accurate. Christmas is a Christian holiday that celebrates the birth of Jesus. Hanukkah has nothing to do with Jesus or with Christianity. Judaism is a much older religion than Christianity.

Purim—
Costumes and Stories

Purim usually falls in March. Purim celebrates the story of Esther in the Bible. Esther was a good and beautiful Jewish woman married to the Persian king, Ahasuerus. Many Jews lived in Persia at this time, but the king did not know that Esther was Jewish. Esther was an orphan and had been raised by her uncle, Mordecai.

Esther's Uncle Mordecai, a particularly good and honest man, heard two of the king's servants planning to kill King Ahasuerus. He warned Esther, who told the king. The servants were caught and punished.

An evil nobleman, Haman, wanted everyone to bow down to him. Mordecai refused, saying that Jews bow only to God. Haman became so angry that he plotted to kill all the Jews in the kingdom. He chose the day for the slaughter by drawing lots. (*Purim* means lots in Hebrew.) And he built a tall gallows to hang Mordecai.

Mordecai told Esther, who went to see the king. This was dangerous. In those days, no one, not even his wife, could talk to the king unless invited. If someone did, the king could order him or her killed! But because Esther was so beautiful, the king just asked her what she wanted. She invited the king and Haman to dinner. At dinner, she asked them to come back in two nights.

On the night in between the two dinners, the king was reading his record book. He came across the story of how Mordecai had saved his life and realized he had never rewarded Mordecai. So he asked Haman for advice: "What should I do for a man I want to honor greatly?"

Haman thought he was going to be honored. He told the king to dress the man in a royal robe and have him ride the king's own horse through the city. He said that someone should walk alongside announcing to everyone that the king was honoring this man. The king said: "Excellent! Now, you go and do that for Mordecai." So instead of hanging Mordecai, Haman had to lead his horse!

At the second dinner, Esther told the king that she was Jewish. She said an evil man wanted to kill all her people and that the man was Haman. The king got very angry. He had Haman hanged from the gallows Haman had built for Mordecai. And he gave orders that the Jews could fight back and kill their enemies. And that's what they did.

That is the story of Purim. This story is read in synagogue on Purim. When Haman's name is read, people boo and stamp their feet. They rattle noisemakers called groggers. Purim is also a time for music, carnivals, plays, and parades. People dress up in masks and costumes to look like characters in the story.

Feasting and drinking wine are part of the Purim celebration. Three-cornered cookies filled with poppy seeds, prunes, and nuts are the special foods for this holiday. In the United States, these treats are usually called *hamantaschen,* or Haman's pockets. In Israel they are called *oznei Haman,* and in Italy they are called *orecchi di Haman*—both meaning Haman's ears!

On Purim, people also give gifts to friends and neighbors. Most gifts are food, like hamantaschen, cakes and other sweets, and fruit. Also gifts of food and money are given to the poor.

Many of the Jewish holiday celebrations take place in synagogues like the one pictured here.

Pesach—Passover

Pesach, or Passover, is one of the most important Jewish holidays. Passover is celebrated at home although special services are given in temple as well. It lasts for eight days and usually takes place in April. Like all Jewish holidays, it begins at sunset, which by Jewish tradition is when a new day begins.

Passover celebrates the exodus of the Jewish people from Egypt. But this is more than the story of the move from one country to another. It is also a story of liberation. In leaving Egypt, the Jewish people went from slavery to freedom.

More than 3,000 years ago in Egypt, there lived an important Jewish official named Joseph. Joseph was a wise man. His dreams warned him of a coming famine. He told the Egyptian pharaoh (king) about the dreams, and the Egyptians stored up food for the hard years ahead. During the famine, Joseph's father and eleven brothers moved to Egypt. Their descendants became the Jewish people.

Many years passed. Joseph and his brothers died. Eventually a new pharaoh decided that there were too many Jews in Egypt. First he made them slaves. The Jews had to work hard making bricks and building palaces for the Egyptians. Then the pharaoh ordered that their newborn baby boys be killed.

Yochevet was a brave Jewish woman. She already had two children, Aaron and Miriam. When she gave birth to a baby boy, she kept him hidden for as long as she could. Then she put him in a basket of reeds. His sister, Miriam, put the baby and basket in the Nile River. Miriam hid behind the river reeds and watched. Soon the pharaoh's daughter came to the river to bathe. She found the baby! She decided to keep him and called him Moses. Miriam told the pharaoh's daughter that she knew of a good nurse. She ran home to get her mother. So Moses' real mother ended up being his nurse in the palace of the Egyptian princess.

When Moses grew up, he saw an Egyptian slave driver beating a Jewish man. He killed the slave driver and then fled into the desert. There, he became a shepherd, got married, and had a son. One day while he was taking care of his sheep, Moses saw a burning bush. The fire kept burning but the bush did not burn up. Moses drew closer and heard the voice of God. God told him to go back to Egypt and tell the pharaoh to let his people go.

Moses was afraid, but he did as God ordered. The pharaoh refused to let the Jews go, so God sent ten plagues to the Egyptians. First, all the water turned to blood. Then frogs came, covering the whole country. Then came lice, flies, cattle disease, boils, hail, locusts, and darkness. Still the pharaoh would not let the Jews go.

Finally God said he would kill the firstborn in every Egyptian house. He gave Moses special instructions for the Jewish people. Each family was to kill and eat a lamb and to sprinkle the lamb's blood on the doorpost of the home. That way the angel who was to kill the Egyptian firstborns would see the blood and pass over the Jewish homes. That is why this holiday is called Passover.

After that night of death, the pharaoh let the Jews leave, and they hurried out of Egypt. But then the pharaoh changed his mind and sent an army after them. God parted the waters of the Red Sea to let the Jews go through it. God let the waters flow back over the Egyptians, drowning them. The Jews escaped and became a free people.

This special celebration marks the end of slavery and the beginning of freedom. Non-Jewish people, too, love the story because it says that God is on the side of the poor and oppressed. The celebration of Passover centers on a special meal called the *seder*. During the seder, families recall both the time of slavery in Egypt and the exodus.

A Jewish family in Israel celebrates the seder meal.

The Seder—
Special Meal and Story

The seder lasts for hours. It includes special stories, songs, and foods. The Haggadah is a special book that has all the prayers, questions, songs, and stories for the seder meal. Family and friends gather for this home celebration. Even non-religious Jews celebrate the message of liberation from oppression.

A group of Orthodox Jews in Israel prepare a kosher meal.

Each kind of food eaten during the seder has special meaning. Most of these foods are arranged on a ceremonial plate. The plate has places for karpas, maror, a roasted egg, a meat bone, haroset, and saltwater. Another plate holds three matzot, covered with a cloth or napkin. Wine, and sometimes grape juice for children, is also on the table. There is one extra wine glass.

Karpas is a green vegetable, like parsley, which is dipped in saltwater and eaten. Green symbolizes new life in spring. The saltwater reminds people of the tears of the Jewish people in slavery.

Maror is a bitter vegetable like horseradish. It is eaten to remember the bitterness of slavery.

A roasted egg is a reminder of animal sacrifice in the years of the Jerusalem Temple.

The meat bone is a reminder of the lamb that was eaten on the night of the first Passover. Some families roast a lamb shank bone. Others use a chicken neck or wing.

Haroset is a delicious mixture of nuts, apples, sugar, and red wine although the recipe varies from family to family. Because of its texture, haroset is a reminder of the clay that the Jewish people used to make bricks during slavery days in Egypt.

Matzot (the plural of matzoh) are a little like crackers. They are made of unleavened bread and are eaten throughout the time of Passover. Leavening is anything—like yeast—that can make baked food rise. Unleavened bread is eaten because at the first Passover the Jews had to leave Egypt so fast that they had no time to let their bread rise. Matzot are eaten at special times during the storytelling and meal. At different parts of the seder they are eaten with horseradish, with haroset, or in a sandwich with both horseradish and haroset.

One small piece of a matzoh is broken off and hidden. This is called the afikomen. After the seder ritual and the dinner are over, children search for the afikomen. Whoever finds it gets a reward.

A table setting for a seder

Tradition says that no leavening (called hametz) can be allowed in Jewish homes during Passover. Before the days of Passover begin, the house must be cleaned of all bread, cereal, cookies, spaghetti, and anything else that contains hametz.

Wine is an important part of the seder meal, as it is of every holiday meal. People drink four glasses of wine at different times during the blessings and the storytelling.

Legend says that the prophet Elijah will one day return. So an extra wine glass is filled for the prophet Elijah and a door is opened to let him come in.

Passover is a time of great storytelling and feasting. The most important part of the holiday is found in the story of the exodus of the Jewish people from slavery in Egypt.

Shavuot— The Feast of Weeks

Shavuot is celebrated seven weeks after Passover. That is why it is called the Feast of Weeks. Like Sukkot, it is, in part, a harvest festival, celebrating the wheat harvest. But it also celebrates a religious event—the giving of the Ten Commandments to Moses and, more generally, the giving of religious laws and the Torah to the Jewish people.

The Torah's story of Ruth, which concerns harvests, is read on Shavuot. Another custom calls for eating dairy foods, such as cheese, ice cream, and blintzes, a kind of pancake filled with sweet cottage cheese. In the United States, people often decorate their homes with flowers and greens for this holiday. In Italy, Jewish people decorate with roses and call this day the Feast of Roses. One story says that Mount Sinai was covered with roses when God gave the Ten Commandments to Moses.

Burning bread before Passover

Days of Mourning

Tishah B'Av is observed in July or August. It commemorates the destruction of the Jerusalem Temple in 587 B.C.E. and in 70 C.E. (B.C.E. means "before the common era" and C.E. means "common era." The common era is when our present, Roman calendar began with the year one. Sometimes people use B.C. and A.D. to mark years "before Christ" and "anno Domini," or "in the year of our Lord." B.C. and A.D. are based on a Christian religious belief, but B.C.E. and C.E. are more neutral ways of dating.)

About 70 years after the first destruction of the Jerusalem Temple by the Babylonians in 587 B.C.E., Jews were allowed to return to Jerusalem and rebuild it. But the Second Temple of Jerusalem was destroyed by the Romans in about 70 C.E. and never rebuilt. Because this Temple was an important center of Judaism, its destruction is still mourned today. Tishah B'Av is observed by fasting and prayer.

Yom Ha-Shoah is a day in late April or May set aside to mourn the Holocaust. The Holocaust happened during the 1930s and 1940s in Europe. The Nazis, led by Adolf Hitler, became the rulers of Germany and then invaded other countries in Europe. They wanted to kill all the Jews in the world. Jews were rounded up and put in concentration camps. There they were shot or gassed and their bodies were burned. By the time the Holocaust ended, six million Jews had been killed. Six million people from other groups were exterminated as well. Some people observe Yom Ha-Shoah with special prayers and fasting. Some observe it by retelling the stories of the Holocaust, and others observe it by keeping silent.

Life-Cycle Celebrations

Naming the Baby

Jewish religious tradition requires that all boys be circumcised eight days after they are born. *Circumcision* means cutting the foreskin away from the penis. In the United States, this is a common medical procedure for many baby boys. For non-Jewish boys, it is frequently done by a doctor in the hospital soon after they are born. For Jewish baby boys, however, the circumcision is done eight days after birth at a special naming celebration called a brit or bris.

Today, the bris may take place at home or in a synagogue or temple. Friends and relatives are invited. A specially trained man—a mohal—performs the small operation, and at the same time the baby boy is named.

For many centuries, girls were not counted as very important in Jewish religious observance, although it was acknowledged that they had an important role in the home. There were no special ceremonies for baby girls. The father simply went to the synagogue or temple soon after his daughter was born and included her name in a prayer of blessing. Today, a more formal celebration is possible in many synagogues and temples. Relatives and friends may be invited, and both parents name the baby.

No celebration is complete without food. After the bris, or naming ceremony, the parents host a meal or a festive kiddush. A kiddush is the name for both the prayer recited over wine and for a festive lunch served after religious services.

Jews in Israel celebrate a young boy's bar mitzvah.

Members of a Jewish community gather together for bar mitzvahs and bat mitzvahs.

Bar Mitzvah, Bat Mitzvah

When does a child become an adult? That is hard to say, but becoming a teenager is a significant step in growing up. This step is marked by a special celebration known as *bar mitzvah* (for boys) or *bat mitzvah* (for girls). The bat mitzvah is a more recent ceremony, since for centuries it was not considered necessary for girls to have this kind of ceremony to mark their becoming adults.

Bar mitzvah means son of the commandment and *bat mitzvah* means daughter of the commandment. Since Judaism is based on observing the commandments, these ceremonies signify becoming a grown-up part of the Jewish religious community.

The Torah contains all of the commandments. It is the holiest part of the Bible, the first five books, and is read at every Jewish religious service. The Torah was originally written in Hebrew. Jewish boys and girls attend Hebrew school to learn to read the Torah.

A bar or bat mitzvah usually takes place when a boy or girl becomes thirteen. It is celebrated in the synagogue or temple, with the boy or girl taking a special part by reading from the Torah. Other family members may also have a special part in the service. Then there is a big party.

The boy or girl usually receives many gifts on this special day. Then he or she can observe tzedekah by giving some of what has been received to charity.

Weddings

Weddings are another important event in the life of a community, as well as in the lives of the bride and groom. Jewish wedding customs include the chuppah, the ketubah, and the wine glass.

The chuppah is a wedding canopy, brightly decorated with cloth and flowers. The bride and groom stand under this canopy during the ceremony.

The ketubah is a contract. In very old times, the bride was purchased by the groom's family. The ketubah set out the terms of the sale. Today, the ketubah is an agreement between the bride and groom. Sometimes it has very traditional language, and sometimes the couple writes their own agreement. Both of them sign it at the wedding.

During a Jewish wedding, a couple stands under a canopy as their friends and family gather around them.

The ketubah is read during a Jewish wedding ceremony.

The bride and groom both drink from a single wine glass at the end of the ceremony. Then the groom smashes it with his foot. This custom has many explanations. Today, the most common explanation is that breaking the glass is a way to remember the ancient destruction of the Jerusalem Temple.

When Someone Dies— Sitting Shiva

Jews are usually buried the day after they die, after a short funeral service. As soon as the person is buried, the family begins a time of mourning known as shiva. Shiva usually lasts one week. The immediate family members do not work or go to school, but instead stay at home. Friends and relatives come to the home to sit with them (sitting shiva) and comfort them. They join in saying the kaddish, special prayers for the dead. They bring food so the family will not have to cook.

Mourning continues for a year after the death of a loved one. During this time, some people go to synagogue or temple daily to say kaddish. Others go just at special times—during the first 30 days or at the end of the year.

The anniversary of a person's death is called the *Yahrzeit* by Ashkenazic Jews. It is called *Annos* by Sephardic Jews. On this day, a lamp or candle is lit at sundown and kept burning until the following day at sunset.

Women traditionally say a special blessing as they light the Sabbath candles.

Blessings Old and New

Blessings, called *berakot*, are very important in Jewish prayer and celebration. Some people say there is a blessing, or berakah for every occasion under the sun—for waking, for going to sleep, for coming in, for going out, for eating, for fasting.

Jewish prayers and blessings are usually written in Hebrew. Hebrew uses a different alphabet than English. When Hebrew words are written in the English (really Roman) alphabet, they are spelled

The Torah contains the commandments and, to Jews, is the
holiest part of the Bible.

according to the way they sound. This is called transliteration. Sometimes the same word is transliterated in more than one way. For example, the Hebrew word for the Festival of Lights is sometimes transliterated as "Hanukkah" and sometimes as "Chanukah."

Here are a few often-used blessings, along with English translations.

Blessing for Lighting the Candles on the Sabbath

Baruch ata adonai, eloheynu melech ha-olam, asher kidshanu
 b'mitzvotav vitzivanu l'hadlik ner shel Shabbat.

Blessed are You, O Lord our God, King of the universe, Who
 sanctified us by Your laws and commanded us to kindle the
 Sabbath light.

A special blessing is recited as candles are lit.

Blessing of the Children on the Sabbath

(For sons) Y'simcha elohim k'Ephraim v'che-Menasheh. Y'varechcha adonai v'yish'mrecha. Ya'er adonai panav eylecha vichunecha. Yisa adonai panav eylecha, v'ya-seym l'cha shalom.

May God make you like Ephraim and Menasheh. The Lord bless you and keep you. The Lord make His face to shine upon you and be gracious to you. The Lord turn His face to you and give you peace.

(For daughters) Y'simeych elohim k'Sarah, Rivka, Rachel v'Leah. Y'varech-cha adonai v'yish'mrecha. Ya'er adonai panav eylecha vichunecha. Yisa adonai panav eylecha, v'ya-seym l'cha shalom.

May God make you like Sarah, Rebecca, Rachel, and Leah. The Lord bless you and keep you. The Lord make His face to shine upon you and be gracious to you. The Lord turn His face to you and give you peace.

Kiddush—Blessing over Wine

Baruch ata adonai, eloheynu melech ha-olam, borey p'ri ha'gafen.

Blessed are You, O Lord our God, King of the universe, Who creates the fruit of the vine.

Blessing over Bread

Baruch ata adonai, eloheynu melech ha-olam, ha'motzi lechem min ha-aretz.

Blessed are You, O Lord our God, King of the universe, Who brings forth bread from the earth.

In Israel a man carefully copies the words of the Bible.

Prayers, blessings, and gathering together are important parts of the Jewish religion. Here men gather together to say prayers on the bank of the East River in New York.

Today many people object to the language of the prayers, which seems to say that God is a man. Some of them are working on rewriting the blessings. One example:

Blessing over Bread

N'varekh et eyn ha-khayyim ha'motzi lechem min ha-aretz.
Let us bless the wellspring of life that brings forth bread from the earth.

For Further Reading

There are many ways to learn more about Jewish customs. You might ask a Jewish friend to take you to a celebration. Or you might call a synagogue and ask when you can attend a service. You can also read other books, such as:

Burstein, Chaya M. *The Jewish Kids Catalog.* Philadelphia, Pennsylvania: Jewish Publication Society of America, 1983.

Cashman, Greer Fay and Alona Frankel. *Jewish Days and Holidays.* New York: Adama Books, 1986.

Gersh, Harry. *When a Jew Celebrates.* New York: Behrman House, 1971.

Greenfeld, Howard, *Passover.* New York: Holt, Rinehart & Winston, 1978.

—*Rosh Hashana and Yom Kippur.* New York: Holt, Rinehart & Winston, 1979.

Simon, Norma. *Hanukkah.* New York: Thomas Y. Crowell Co., 1966.

Index

Aaron *22*
Abraham *14*
afikomen *26*
Ahasuerus *19*
Annos *37*
Antiochus Epiphanes *17*
Ashkenazic Jews *6, 37*

bar mitzvah, bat mitzvah *5, 32, 33, 34*
berakot, berakah *39*
blintzes *29*
brit, bris *31*
Book of Life *12*

challah *8, 9, 12*
chuppah *34*
circumcision *31*
Conservative *10*
conversion *6*

Days of Awe *10, 12, 13, 17*
dreidl *17*

Elijah *29*
Esther *19, 20*
exodus *22, 23, 29*

Falasha *6*
Feast of Lights *17, 41*
Feast of Roses *29*
Feast of Weeks *29*

Festival of Booths *14*

groggers *20*

Haggadah *24*
Haman *19, 20*
hamantaschen *20*
hametz *27*
Hanukkah *16, 17, 18, 19, 41, 46*
Hanukkah gelt *6, 17*
haroset *26*
Hasidic Jews *9*
Hebrew *5, 6, 9, 10, 14, 17, 19, 34, 39, 41*
High Holy Days *5, 10*
Holocaust *5, 30*

Isaac *14*
Israel *6, 16, 20*

Jerusalem Temple *16, 17, 26, 29, 30, 37*
Joseph *22*

kaddish *37*
karpas *26*
ketubah *34*
kiddush *9, 31, 43*
Kol Nidre *13*

Ladino *6*
latkes *17*

Maccabees *17*
maror *26*
matzoh, matzot *26*
menorah *16, 17*
Miriam *22*
mohal *31*
Mordecai *19, 20*
Moses *14, 22, 23, 29, 30*

observant *9, 13*
orecchi di Haman *20*
Orthodox *7*
oznei Haman *20*

Passover, Pesach *17, 22, 23, 26, 27, 29, 46*
pischke *13*
plagues *23*
Purim *19, 20*

Reconstructionist *10*
Reform *9, 10*
Rosh Hashanah *10, 11, 12, 46*
Ruth *29, 30*

Sabbath, Shabbat, Shabbos *5, 8, 9, 10, 13, 41, 43*
Second Temple *30*
secular *6*
seder *23, 24, 26, 27, 29*
Sephardic Jews *6, 17, 37*
shamash *17*

Shavuot *29, 30*
shiva *37*
shofar *10, 11, 12, 13*
shul *10*
sufganiyot *17*
sukkah *14*
Sukkot *14, 29*
synagogue *5, 9, 10, 14, 20, 31, 34, 37*

temple *5, 9, 10, 14, 16, 17, 22, 29, 30, 31, 34, 37*
tashlikh *12*
Tishah B'Av *30*
Tishri *10, 14*
Torah *34*
tzedekah *13, 34*

weddings *34-37*

Yahrzeit *37*
Yiddish *6*
Yochevet *22*
Yom Ha-Shoah *30*
Yom Kippur *12, 13, 46*